Walter Lloyd

The Galilean

A portrait of Jesus of Nazareth

Walter Lloyd

The Galilean
A portrait of Jesus of Nazareth

ISBN/EAN: 9783337257743

Printed in Europe, USA, Canada, Australia, Japan

Cover: Foto ©Lupo / pixelio.de

More available books at **www.hansebooks.com**

THE GALILEAN:

𝔄 Portrait

OF

JESUS OF NAZARETH.

BY

WALTER LLOYD.

WILLIAMS AND NORGATE,

14, HENRIETTA STREET, COVENT GARDEN, LONDON;

AND

20, SOUTH FREDERICK STREET, EDINBURGH.

1892.

LONDON:
PRINTED BY C. GREEN AND SON,
178, STRAND.

CONTENTS.

—————•◦•—————

I.

INTRODUCTORY.

THE life of Jesus of Nazareth has been written from so many points of view, that it may be thought it is unnecessary to add one more to the number. Yet I cannot help feeling that none that I have read are altogether natural and simple enough to give a true and consistent picture of one of the simplest figures in history. Lives of Jesus written from the orthodox point of view, hide the reality of the person under theological dreams. Immediately we begin to read of him as the King of the Jews, the Messiah, the Redeemer, the Only-begotten Son of God, we leave the world of realities for that of imagination. I have no intention of entering upon any theological discussion ; I am so convinced that Jesus himself was not responsible for the dogmas which have arisen concerning him, that even to enter into a discussion about them would divert attention from the character I wish to portray. For the same reason I have abstained from any detailed review of the manners and customs, especially of a religious nature, of the locality and times.

B

There is no need to repeat what everybody knows. These may be found already to hand in Edersheim, Keim, Hausrath, the various works of Renan, Farrar, and many other authors. But the method which results in expanding the biography of Jesus into several bulky volumes, ends by obscuring the central object of interest, Neither do I discuss at length here the question of miracles, or of the supernatural birth and resurrection ; that they are legendary accretions, I have no manner of doubt. All that we know of the life of the Galilean Teacher is limited to the brief period beginning with the preaching of John the Baptist and ending with the crucifixion. The first three Gospels were written more than a generation after the death of Jesus, and the fourth Gospel much later still ; they are not the work of eye-witnesses, but the reproduction of oral traditions, plentifully mixed with legends which had grown in a natural manner from very slender bases. Still I believe there is sufficient authentic matter embodied in the Gospels to enable us to form a vivid conception of the personality of Jesus ; and often unconsciously the narrators have told us the truth about him, which contradicts the fictions which inconsistently accompany it. A knowledge of human nature and a familiarity with the history of the times, renders it comparatively easy to determine at least what may be true and what must be false. In the same manner we may distinguish, in the reported sayings and teaching of Jesus, between what may have been his actual words, and what in all probability were after-thoughts or glosses considered necessary by his biographers to support their own views of his character and mission ; and in many instances to minimize and limit the unqualified sentiments of a teacher, all but incomprehensible to the Jewish mind. I have, therefore, in the main confined myself, in my endeavour to draw a likeness of Jesus, to what is natural in the Gospels. I might have crowded my pages with quotations and references to authorities ; and though this might have given them the appearance of learning, it would have marred my purpose. I have read and gathered suggestions from a large number of works upon the subject—"authorities" I hesitate to call them, because none of them can give any information at first-hand. For the correction of many prevailing misconceptions, I am indebted more to travellers and explorers than to theologians, though even in this department Josephus must remain the fountain-head of information. I am especially indebted to Stanley's *Sinai and Palestine*, Major Conder's *Palestine*, Sayce's *Hittites*, Kitto's *Scripture Lands*, Manning's *Those Holy Fields*, and Dr. Selah Merrill's *Galilee in the Time of Christ ;* but even from these I quote but sparingly. My aim has been rather to draw a portrait than to write a history, and, by clearing away the accumulations of centuries, to see what manner of man Jesus of Nazareth was. I have not attempted to construct a story, but, by the gathering together of characteristics depicted in the Gospels, have tried to understand the man. The brevity of my sketch is consistent with the subject, and is deliberate; for the public life of the Galilean Teacher was all too short, and the trustworthy records are so brief, that even my short sketch goes far beyond their measure. If I have abstained from the usual eulogizing of my subject, it is not from want of reverence or of gratitude, or because I do not appreciate the debt the world owes to one of its greatest benefactors. It may be thought by some that my picture of Jesus is self-condemned, that it is inadequate to account for what Emerson truly called "the unique impression of Jesus upon mankind." I will also let Emerson serve me with my defence:

> "Love's hearts are faithful, but not fond,
> Bound for the just, but not beyond:
> Not glad, as the low-loving herd,
> Of self in other still preferred,
> But they have heartily designed
> The benefit of broad mankind.
> And they serve men austerely,
> After their own genius, clearly,
> Without a false humility:
> For this is Love's nobility,—
> Not to scatter bread and gold,
> Goods and raiment bought and sold:
> But to hold fast his simple sense,
> And speak the speech of innocence,

Introductory.

And with hand, and body, and blood,
To make his bosom-counsel good.
For he that feeds men serveth few ;
He serves all who dare be true."

The Celestial Love.

II.

JESUS AND THE LAW.

I CANNOT do better than preface my brief study of the life of Jesus of Nazareth with two passages from the English translation of Renan's *Vie de Jésus*, as they will at once open up to us a most important question, to which to some extent, I hope, these pages will give an answer. The first citation is from the first chapter, and the second from the twenty-eighth chapter, of Trübner's edition of the Life of Jesus.

"The great event in the history of the world is the revolution by which the noblest portions of humanity have passed from the ancient religions, comprised under the vague name of Paganism, to a religion founded on the Divine Unity, the Trinity and the Incarnation of the Son of God. It has taken nearly a thousand years to accomplish this conversion ; the new religion had itself taken at least three hundred years in its formation. But the origin of the revolution in question is a fact which took place under the reigns of Augustus and Tiberius. At that time there lived a superior personage, who, by his bold originality, and by the love which he was able to inspire, became the object and fixed the starting-point of the future faith of humanity."

Let us place the following quotation by the side of the above :

"Jesus, it will be seen, limited his action entirely to the Jews. Although his sympathy for those despised by orthodoxy led him to admit pagans into the kingdom of God— although he had resided more than once in a pagan country, and once or twice we surprise him in friendly relations with unbelievers— it may be said that his life was passed entirely in the very restricted world in which he was born."

Embodied in these two statements there is a contradiction which the brilliant author has strangely overlooked and not attempted to explain. If the facts are correctly stated, we have a curious problem, not to say a paradox. The one statement is, that Jesus limited his action, confined his preaching and restricted his mission, entirely to the Jews, which is certainly open to question. The other statement is, that it is the pagans who have been converted to Christianity, about which there can be no doubt. So we have these contradictions : that Jesus preached to the Jews, and not to the pagans ; but it is the pagans who have become his followers, and not the Jews. The Jews to whom he preached rejected him, and the pagans whom he avoided have received him. I know there is a theological explanation of this difficulty, which, however, cannot carry weight with the historical critic, and to Paul is attributed the success of Christianity amongst the Gentiles. But it seems a baseless assumption that had the Gospel at first been exclusively meant for and adapted to the Jews, it would have proved so acceptable to the Gentiles. The natural inference would be, that the Gospel originally was more adapted to the Gentiles than to the Jews, if it was not actually presented to them as freely, and that Jesus had drawn his inspiration more from Gentile than from Jewish sources. At least I think I shall be able to show that the religious sentiments of Jesus had been largely influenced by his contact and sympathy with the Gentiles of northern Palestine, and that the world in which he was born, and in which he moved, was not the very restricted one of orthodox Judaism, as even M. Renan would lead us to suppose.

We may arrive at an understanding of the relation of Jesus to the Jews and Judaism by examining his attitude in detail to the Law, to the Jews, to the Gentiles, to Jerusalem ; we may then be led to discover the root of his unquestionable dislike to Judaism, and thus find an answer to the problem I have described.

What was the attitude of Jesus to the Law and teaching of the Jews? It was anti-Jewish—not only in spirit, but in the treatment of details. Not only was he the uncompromising critic of the "traditions of men," which had parasitically added themselves to the "Law of Moses," but he rejected the Law itself, in a purely Gentile spirit. I shall be met at once with the statement that Jesus himself said that he came, not to destroy, but to fulfil the Law. The word fulfil is understood to mean, "to teach and do what the Law requires;" but Jesus meant that his teaching (the Sermon on the Mount) only completed or put the finishing-stroke to the Law, that his spiritual teaching would perfectly accomplish what the Law imperfectly aimed at. Christianity begins where the Law ends. He did not mean that he was orthodox, but that the truth was orthodox, though the application of it would abolish the old orthodoxy. Nevertheless, in enunciating spiritual principles, which virtually amounted to rejecting the traditions and laws of the Jews, he claimed to be teaching the truest and highest religion of Israel— just as a "liberal" Christian in these days, who is not regarded as a Christian by a Catholic, claims to teach the purest Christianity. When Jesus was asked, Which is the greatest commandment? he replied, That which commands us to love God, and next to that, the one which commands us to love our neighbour. True, these are found in the Pentateuch, but they are not part of the Law, of which a Jew would think when he asked the question; any more than if an ecclesiastic now was to ask a student, Which is the greatest Christian doctrine? would he expect as an answer, "Those which are contained in the Sermon on the Mount." Though the ecclesiastic could not deny this, he would add, But it is also necessary for salvation to believe

all the doctrines and fulfil all the commands of the
Church.   So the Jewish author of the first Gospel,
alarmed at what might be the consequence to the Law
of the broad application of the words of Jesus, adds :
" For verily I say unto you, till heaven and earth pass
away, one jot or one tittle shall in no wise pass away
from the Law until all shall be accomplished.   Whosoever, therefore, shall break one of the least com-
mandments and shall teach men so, shall be called
least in the kingdom of heaven ; but whosoever shall
do and teach them, shall be called great in the kingdom
of heaven."   This is in direct contradiction to the
teaching of Jesus, but it is only one, and perhaps the
most important, instance of a frequent practice on the
part of the Evangelists in their endeavour to reconcile
the teaching of Jesus with Judaism ; they were not
able to realize that their Master had intentionally
spoken heresy.   They qualified and often destroyed
the force of his sayings by an explanation of their
own.*

It is not necessary to give many instances of the
antipathy of Jesus to the Law, as it is evident through-
out the Gospels ; from one or two cases we may form
a judgment of the whole subject.   As a crucial test,

---

* The transition from the words of Jesus to the gloss of his
commentator, for such the writer really is, may frequently be
traced by the particle "for."   See *The Three First Gospels*,
J. E. Carpenter, M.A., 2nd edition, p. 394.

we may refer to the observance of the Sabbath as best illustrating the principle by which we find Jesus was animated. The rigid observance of the Sabbath by the strict Jews, and the multiplicity of rules in vogue, are too well known to need repeating in this place—an elaborate account of them may be found in Edersheim's *Life of Jesus;* what I wish to point out is, that Jesus went behind all these laws and customs to first principles, to man and his needs, and the evident dictates of nature. This is proved by the far-reaching dictum which he pronounced in controversy on the point, that "the Sabbath was made for man, and not man for the Sabbath;" that the end and aim of legislation and religious custom should be the sole object of conducing to the well-being of man; that the laws had no other *raison d'être.* They were not to be regarded as arbitrary expressions of the Divine Will, to be submitted to under every condition, but they were themselves to be submitted to the requirements of human life. He appealed to the laws of Nature against the Law of Moses. Nothing could have been further from the Jewish way of thinking than this. According to the Jews, man might suffer or perish, but the Law must not be broken. The magnitude of the difference in the view of Jesus on the subject and that of the orthodox Jews, is seen in the fact that it was the Sabbath question which first provoked their animosity: the number of cases in

which this appears, however unhistoric they may be
in some of their details, leaves no room for doubt as
to the reality of the source.   In one instance in the
fourth Gospel, Jesus is also reported to have met the
objections to his way of regarding the Sabbath by
the enunciation of another principle in consonance
with nature.   The reason given by the Jews for the
abstinence from work on the Sabbath was, that in six
days the Lord made heaven and earth, the sea and all
that in them is, and rested the seventh day.   Jesus
put this, which was a fundamental part of the Jewish
cosmogony, on one side, saying, " My Father worketh
until now, and I work."   This recognition of the con-
tinuity of creation, of the unceasing activity of God,
practically an identification of God with Nature, was **a**
Gentile and not a Jewish conception ; indeed, it was
so incomprehensible to the Jews, that we are told that
for this cause they sought the more to kill him, because
he not only brake the Sabbath, but also called God his
Father, making himself equal with God.   In his conceptions of God and man and nature, Jesus appeared
to have nothing in common with the Jews.

Another instance illustrating the same principle
may be found in his treatment of the question of
marriage and divorce.   The marriage question was a
burning one just then, owing to the conduct of Herod,
and the outspokenness of John the Baptist on the
subject had cost him his head.   So that when the

Jews asked Jesus, " Is it lawful for a man to put away his wife ?" it appears as if, by that apparently simple question, a trap was laid for him, which he ingeniously avoided. Turning to the Pharisees, he asked what their own lawgiver had commanded. Moses, said they, commanded to give a bill of divorcement and to put her away. Moses, said he, for your hardness of heart, suffered you to put away your wives. All Moses did was to introduce some regulations for the better protection of wives, and at least to command that a man should not. put away his wife without some show of cause and without some legal form. But even this afforded little protection to the woman, and gave unbounded liberty to the man. Even Josephus says of himself without any qualification: "About the same time I forsook my wife, because her manner pleased me not, although she was the mother of my three children." But Jesus faced the question by an appeal to nature, which by inference he declared no law of Moses could override. " Have ye not read that from the beginning he made them male and female, and the twain shall become one flesh, so that they are no more twain but one. What, therefore, God (or Nature) hath joined together, let not man put asunder." This pleased even the disciples so little that they said : " If the case of the man is so with his wife, it is better not to marry." Here, then, as with the Sabbath question, we find Jesus substituting a broad generalization, based upon nature, for the narrow and selfish laws of the Jews, which they believed or chose to think of Divine authority. The only authority to Jesus was the constitution of the world as he conceived it. In principle we can find nothing broader than this; it is a test that even we are slow to apply to laws and customs sanctioned by their antiquity, however little they may be in accordance with the real interests of society. We may apply the principle which appears in the treatment of these two great fundamental subjects to the way in which Jesus regarded the whole conduct of life, and we find in almost every point he was at variance with the Jews. They appealed to "the Law;" he appealed to nature and human nature. Fasts, ablutions, prayers, alms, the treatment of those who injure us, the innermost springs of conduct, were all looked at by him, not as a Jew would look, but as a wise and high-minded Gentile would regard them.

Renan says that "Jesus did not speak against the Mosaic Law; but it is clear that he saw its insufficiency, and allowed it to be seen that he did so." "A pure worship, a religion without priests and external observances, resting entirely on the feelings of the heart, on the imitation of God, on the direct relation of the conscience with the Heavenly Father, was the result of these principles. Jesus never shrank from this bold conclusion, which made him a thorough revolutionist in the centre of Judaism." We can, perhaps,

now begin to see how it was that Jesus made so little
impression on the Jews, but, when he became wider
known, was received with gladness by the Gentiles.
He had everything in common with them; he had
nothing in common with the Jews.   It is difficult to
believe that his conception of religion was in any way
derived from the Jews; it is easy to believe that it was
largely due to Gentile influence.   He was altogether
out of place among the Pharisees; he would have
been at home with the Stoics.

III.

JESUS AND THE JEWS.*

———◦•◦———

In the last chapter I have noticed the attitude of Jesus towards the Law of Moses, and have seen, not only his indifference to the traditions and rules of the Rabbis, but his assertion of the supremacy of the natural rights of man even over the supposed sacred Law itself. With regard to the Sabbath, to divorce and marriage, sacrifices, gifts, fasts and everything peculiarly Jewish, he opposed broad humanity to national prejudice. He asserted the superiority of man, as man, over anything that had been laid down in the name of the great Lawgiver. To put it briefly, what had been necessary and expedient in early times had to be adjusted to a wider conception of humanity and a loftier idea of God. And he did not hesitate

---

* By the "Jews" I wish it to be distinctly understood that I refer only to the followers of the Priestly Code, which was developed after the exile, and more especially after the Maccabean struggle. This must be distinguished from the earlier and loftier religion of Israel's greatest prophets. In the time of Jesus I regard this "Judaism" as especially the religion of the Priests, Pharisees and Scribes, who had their head-quarters in Jerusalem.

to say that the day was passed for confining the spirit of man by the old bands of ancient laws.

We now turn to another topic closely associated with this one, and that is the attitude of Jesus to the Jews of his own day. The two topics are naturally related. The Jews, socially and religiously, were to a certain extent the product of their Law. The law a man obeys and reverences moulds his character. The Law had grown in days when it was thought necessary, by the theocratic spirit of their rulers, to separate the Israelites from the surrounding people, by discouraging intercourse and marriage with them, and encouraging customs and practices which at any rate they believed to be peculiar to themselves. The possession and observance of these laws, based as they believed them to be upon divine authority, led them to think of themselves as a people peculiarly dear to the Most High, and fostered a feeling of isolation and pride which made them assume an air of superiority over those whom they called the heathen. This naturally developed into a narrowness and bigotry that earned for them the description of being haters of mankind. They kept themselves to themselves, and held aloof from people of other nationalities.

Their ceremonial religion fostered formality and hypocrisy. This is perfectly natural, and a universal consequence of ceremonialism. If religion is supposed

C

to consist in the performance of certain rites and the observance of ceremonies, and obedience to external rules, those who are most strict in their observances and obedience will consider themselves the most religious, and in their zeal for a formal religion will gradually increase the number of rites and ceremonies, and become ever more busy in the multiplication of restrictions.

Yet all the time their conduct and character may be unimproved ; and they thus earn for themselves the reputation of hypocrites. If the men who are most strict in the observance of the Sabbath, in the payment of tithes, in the repetition of prayers, in outward observances with regard to ablutions, dress and fasts, are at the same time immoral, extortionate, uncharitable, the name of hypocrite is not undeserved. It is not to be wondered at that other men, who care little for ceremonial religion, but something for mercy and justice, for purity of life and a charitable disposition, should treat their assumption of superior righteousness with scorn, and their vices with indignation.

This, I think, will go far to explain the attitude of Jesus to the Jews of his own day.

On the one hand, we find a class of men devoted to a formal religion, but indifferent to spiritual religion, and neglectful of their first duties to humanity. On the other hand, we find a spiritually-minded man utterly indifferent to the punctilious observance of a wearisome and unsympathetic formalism, but over-flowing with generosity and a love for man.

This difference will explain to us the severe con-demnation passed by Jesus upon the Jews, and it explains at the same time the irritation and anger the Jews felt towards Jesus. That his condemnation was just and unanswerable, only made it sting the Pharisees more keenly.

We can form a picture of the character of the Jews in the time of Jesus from the Gospels themselves, which is probably all the more accurate because the effect appears to have been unintentional. I speak of the Jews in general, and not merely of the priests or Pharisees, though the characteristics of the race may have been most marked in them. What is said pro-bably applies more particularly to the Jews of Jeru-salem and the neighbourhood, rather than to those scattered over other parts of the country. The dif-ference between the Galileans and the Judæans I must describe more fully in another chapter, but there was a difference very deep and very marked. In the fourth Gospel the Jews are constantly described as being opposed to Jesus, who is never called a Jew, but a Galilean ; and all the apostles, except one, were Galileans, that one being the remarkable exception of Judas Iscariot, the man of Kerioth. The importance of that exception we shall see presently.

The general character of the orthodox Jews is
easily summed up in the language we find in the
Gospels. They loved to make a show of their religion. They dressed in a peculiar manner, wore long
clothing, and made their phylacteries broad. They
were excessively punctilious in their observance of
the Sabbath. They prayed in public; they made a
virtue of their unnecessary zeal in tithing themselves,
and in fasting and almsgiving—to be seen of men;
they not only fasted, but took care that they appeared
unto others to fast. They called attention in every
possible way to their performance of religious rites:
"I fast twice a week; I give tithes of all that I
possess."

And yet with all their zeal they had no spirit of
humanity or mercy; they devoured widows' houses
and for a pretence made long prayers. The religion
of Jerusalem was an organized hypocrisy, at which the
soul of the simple-minded Nazarene revolted. The
prevailing sin was the love of money. The same word
is used by Luke as by the author of the Epistle to
Timothy, when he says the " love of money is the root
of all evil ;" when Jesus was preaching the necessity of
generosity and renunciation, Luke says the Pharisees,
who were lovers of money (φιλάργυροι), derided him.
In the Gospel of Luke, we find John the Baptist is
described as attacking this particular vice. When the
people asked him what they should do, he answered'

Let him that hath two coats impart to him that hath none; and he that hath meat, let him do likewise; which is as much as to say that their besetting sin was selfishness. The publicans said, What shall we do? He answered, Exact no more than that which is appointed you. Their besetting sin was extortion. The soldiers said, What shall we do? Do violence to no man, neither accuse any man falsely, and be content with your wages. Here, again, coveteousness was the cause of misconduct. The soldiers committed robbery with violence; they made false accusations for the purpose of obtaining black-mail, and all because they were not content with their wages. Truly, the love of money was the root of all evils. Judas Iscariot was the only Jew amongst the twelve, and he betrayed his Master for money. When the woman anointed Jesus with costly ointment, he said, Why was not this sold for three hundred pence and given to the poor? This he said, writes the Evangelist, with frightful severity, not because he cared for the poor, but because he was a thief and carried the bag.

It is often thought that Jesus commended poverty for its own sake, and that those are his most faithful followers who abandon the world and its occupations, and devote themselves to a life of poverty. At first sight this may appear justified by many things which Jesus is reported to have said; but when we realize when they were said, why they were said, and to

whom they were said, we may better appreciate his
intention. They were addressed to those to whom
the love of money, and therefore money itself, was a
curse. It had driven all humanity out of their hearts,
and had bred a generation of hypocrites such as,
happily, the world has seldom seen. It is in the
light of this circumstance that we must interpret the
sayings of the Galilean Teacher: such as, "How hardly
shall they that have riches enter into the kingdom of
heaven;" "Take heed and beware of covetousness,
for a man's life consisteth not in the things which he
hath;" "Yet one thing thou lackest—sell all that thou
hast and give it to the poor."

This love of money had entered into the very pre-
cincts of the temple and infected its worship; religion
itself was turned into a source of profit. "My house
shall be called the house of prayer, but ye have made
it a den of thieves."

Jesus himself, heart and soul, was opposed to this
covetous spirit of the Jews; it drove him, as a gene-
rous-minded man, to the other extreme, and he lauded
liberality as the first of human virtues, and the nearest
approach to the perfection of God. He came from
almost a different world amongst the generous-hearted
Galileans, whose free spirit resembled the profuse
generosity of nature in their native province, while the
stony-hearted Jews had grown like the barren mountains and deserts of Judæa. He said, Set no store

upon riches; have no anxiety for the morrow; give to every one that asketh of thee—give, and it shall be given unto you. While the Jews were saying, "Get all you can," Jesus said, "Give all you can;" and so true it is that with the same measure you mete it shall be measured to you again, that the narrow and exclusive and selfish Jews have been cast out by all nations; the generous, careless-hearted Galilean has been adored as the darling of mankind.

His great-hearted generosity was seen in another direction, in his treatment of Gentiles and sinners; but that must be treated in another chapter; but he said that the Jews were further from the kingdom of heaven than the sinners and heathen they despised. And the reason is not far to seek, if the character given to them in the Gospels had any foundation in fact; but that there does not seem any possible reason to doubt.

IV.

JESUS AND JERUSALEM.

—•+•—

ONE of the curious illusions that has clung to Christianity through so many centuries is the notion that the purest religion of Israel was to be found in Jerusalem, and that out of the religion of Jerusalem Christianity sprang. And not only the Jews, but Christians have looked upon Jerusalem as the ideal city and the type of the kingdom of heaven. They forget that in the book of Revelation, from which the idea has largely been derived, it is the *New Jerusalem* which is spoken of, and not Jerusalem in Judæa. Although the writer, himself a Jew, adopted the familiar name, the ideas associated with it were the reverse of those associated with the Jewish metropolis. It was the New Jerusalem that in a vision he saw descending from heaven, in which should not enter anything unclean, or abominable, or false. The real Jerusalem, which was the enemy of the spirit which gave birth to Christianity, was full of abominations and lies. The same writer describes it as that great city which spiritually is called Sodom and Egypt, where also the

Lord was crucified. The Christianity of the Apocalypse is only a purified Judaism; it speaks of the blasphemy of those who say they are Jews and are not; and in the new earth precedence is to be given to the twelve tribes of Israel. This will explain why the writer selected Jerusalem as the name for the ideal city of God.

How deeply-rooted the idea is that Christianity owes its origin to Jerusalem, may be inferred from the fact that even the late Professor Clifford, who rejected all forms of Christianity, says in one of his essays, in denouncing sacerdotal Christianity and explaining its genesis: " The Gospel indeed came out of Judæa, but the Church and her dogmas came out of Egypt." Wherever the Church came from, whether from Egypt or Greece or Rome, one thing is certain, that the Gospel did not come out of Judæa; Rabbinism came of Judæa, but the Gospel came out of Galilee.

There was nothing in common between the religion of Jesus and that of Jerusalem. In the free and open air, and independent and unfettered thought of Galilee, Jesus had learned to believe in the spirituality of religion—in mercy, love, purity and meekness, being greater than the Law; but when he came to Jerusalem, he found a religion with which he had no sympathy, which at first filled him with disappointment, and ultimately with indignation.

It seems probable that until he had reached man-

hood he had never been in Jerusalem. The story
that he had been there when a boy and disputed even
then with the doctors in the temple, can only be
looked upon as an interesting legend.

When Jesus led his disciples up to Jerusalem, they
were amazed and afraid—amazed at his daring, and
afraid of the reception they might meet.   They knew
enough to perceive that there was not the toleration
in Jerusalem that prevailed in Galilee, and that there
he would encounter an opposition and hostility which
they would rather not incur.

I say, I think he was a stranger in Jerusalem.   On
the occasion of his first visit, some of his companions
called his attention to the buildings of the temple :
" Master, behold what manner of stones and what
manner of buildings!" Just the language that strangers
from the provinces would use when they first caught
sight of the magnificent buildings of the metropolis.
They were evidently struck with admiration at all
this grandeur to which they were unaccustomed.   But
the impression made upon Jesus was very different.
He had received amongst the hills of Galilee, and in
the beautiful garden of Gennesaret by the side of the
lake, that spiritual and poetic insight which made
him feel the littleness and the insubstantiality of the
most splendid works of man.   " See ye not all these
things : verily I say unto you, there shall be left here
one stone upon another that shall not be thrown

down." It was not in the literal sense a prophecy of
the destruction of Jerusalem ; it was simply the wider
sweep of a great imagination that looked through the
shows of time and saw the eternal realities beyond.
Not unlike the emotion which moved Shakespeare
when he wrote :

> " The cloud-capt towers, the gorgeous palaces,
> The solemn temples, the great globe itself,
> Yea, all which it inherit, shall dissolve,
> And like this insubstantial pageant faded,
> Leave not a rack behind."

Some such thought possessed the mind of Jesus as
he gazed upon the splendid buildings and gorgeous
decorations of the temple of the Jews : a sentiment
which took another turn in the mind of the fourth
Evangelist when he said—"The hour cometh when
neither in this mountain nor in Jerusalem shall ye
worship the Father," but when the true temple would
be the human heart.

Jerusalem had an evil reputation even in the days
of Isaiah. It was to the inhabitants of Jerusalem he
said, after calling it Sodom and Gomorrah : "Your
hands are full of blood. Wash you, make you clean.
Put away the evil of your doings from before mine
eyes. Cease to do evil, learn to do well. Seek judgment, set right the oppressor, judge the fatherless,
plead for the widow ;" and in the same breath he
condemned all the gorgeous formalities of their sacri-

ficial religion. The inhabitants of the city retained their characteristics until the end.

The sight of Jerusalem, instead of filling Jesus with enthusiasm, only aroused in him the most painful memories. " O Jerusalem, Jerusalem ; thou that killest the prophets and stonest them that are sent unto thee !" The Jews about him whom he saw, and who would not receive his message, were the children of those that killed the prophets : and though they adorned the sepulchres of the martyrs, their spirit was the same as that of their ancestors. As their fathers did, so did they.

" There was a man that was a householder which planted a vineyard, and set a hedge about it, and digged a wine-press in it, and built a tower, and let it out to husbandmen, and went into another country. And when he sent his servants to receive the fruits, they beat one, and killed another, and stoned another. And when he sent his son, they said, This is the heir ; come, let us kill him." The vineyard was Jerusalem ; the servants were the prophets ; the husbandmen were the Jews. " When the chief-priests and the Pharisees heard his parables, they perceived that he spake of *them.*"

A striking parallel to the visit of the young Galilean to Jerusalem is to ·be found in the visit of young Luther to Rome. Only perhaps Luther expected more of Rome than Jesus did of Jerusalem.

"As soon as Luther entered Rome, he fell on his knees and raised his hands to heaven, and exclaimed, Hail! holy Rome! In his enthusiasm he hastened to every sacred spot, saw all and believed all. But he soon discovered he was the only believer. Christianity seemed to be forgotten in the capital of the Christian world."* "He found in Italy," says Michelet, "a characteristic of which history has seldom or never presented another instance—in a word, the priest atheist." I fear that history has witnessed too many instances of the kind. Jesus found the same thing in Jerusalem—the unbelieving priests, the generation of hypocrites. And we might say he was the only believer in Moses in the capital of the Mosaic religion. The Scribes and Pharisees sat in Moses' seat, and the temple was a den of thieves.

In the Gospel according to Matthew, the controversy between Jesus and the Jews is very effectively and dramatically related, and the importance attached to his Galilean origin demonstrated. It was because they knew he was a Galilean, and they knew the indisposition of the Galileans to submit to foreign authority, that they thought it might be possible to entrap him into some admission which would set either the authorities or the populace against him. So the Pharisees, with the Herodians, set upon him with great plausibility: "Master, we know that thou

* Michelet, *Life of Luther*, chap. i.

art true, and teachest the way of God in truth, and carest not for any one. Tell us, therefore, what thinkest thou, is it lawful to give tribute to Cæsar or not?" This was not a chance question, put at haphazard, but an endeavour to find out if he were a follower of, or a sympathizer with, Judas the Gaulanite. When Jesus was a lad, Cyrenius, the Roman senator, was sent into Syria by Cæsar to assess and tax every man's goods. At first the Jews objected to pay the tax, but ultimately submitted under the persuasion of the high-priest. But a certain Jew, Judas of Gamala, called the Gaulanite, as Gamala was a town in Gaulanitis, arose and stirred up the Galileans to rebel, declaring that the tax was a confession of servitude. Josephus calls the followers of Judas a sect, but they were a politico-religious party. "They were extremely zealous of their liberty, acknowledging but one only God, Lord and Master of all things, and had rather themselves, with their dearest children and kindred, should endure the most grievous and bitter torments that may be imagined, than call any mortal man Lord."* So that when the Pharisees and Herodians asked Jesus if it were lawful to give tribute to Cæsar, they probably hoped he would say it was not, when he might be arrested as a rebel; while if he openly declared it was, it would alienate the Galileans from him. Now there was a saying of the Rabbis, that

* Josephus, *Antiquities*, Bk. xviii.

wherever the coins of a king were in circulation, it was an admission that that king was lord. This is the meaning of the action of Jesus. "Bring me the tribute-money. Whose image and superscription is this?" They say unto him, Cæsar's. Then, said he, render unto Cæsar the things that are Cæsar's. By using his currency, you admit the legality of the tribute.

Then the Sadducees attack him on the question of the future life, on which they differed from the Pharisees. To which he answered with a quotation from the Pentateuch, which they both accepted; and drew this inference—the patriarchs are immortal; for God is not the God of the dead, but of the living.

So then a Scribe came forward and wanted to know which is the greatest commandment. Here, too, was a subject upon which the Jews were always at variance amongst themselves—the relative importance of the commands of the law or tradition. No doubt they expected he would give some answer relating to ceremonial matters which would be sure to give offence to one party or another. But again they had not comprehended the greatness of mind of the man they challenged. "Thou shalt love the Lord thy God with all thy heart," &c.; and though they had not asked for it, he gave them the second great command— "and thy neighbour as thyself." Jesus did not affirm these as original; they were the greatest commands

in the Pentateuch. On these two, he added, hang *all*
the law and the prophets—great and small precepts
alike.

So then Jesus turned upon them with a question—
"What think ye of the Christ, whose son is he? They
say unto him, The son of David. He saith unto
them, How then doth David in the spirit call him
Lord?" quoting what they believed to be a Messianic
psalm written by David himself.

> "The Lord saith unto my Lord,
>   Sit thou on my right hand
>   Till I put thy enemies underneath thy feet."

If David, then, calleth him Lord, how is he his son?
And no one was able to answer him a word. I do
not suppose that Jesus meant to refer to himself or
to any one else as the Messiah in asking these questions; he only wished to take the conceit out of his
inquisitors, and show how utterly ignorant they were
of the meaning of their own Scriptures, and how
absurd was their method of exegesis.

It was then that he turned about upon them, and
let them see that he detected the hypocrisy which lay
beneath their assumed desire to be taught. And it
was after these discourses that the Jews began to
consider how they might put him to death. It is
probable that he then went back for a time to Galilee,
for he would not walk in Judæa, for the Jews sought
to kill him. But before long he said, Let us go into

Judæa again. The disciples said, "Master, the Jews were but now seeking to stone thee, and goest thou thither again?" Why he went we hardly know; he might have felt a necessity laid upon him, a fatalistic feeling which drew him to his doom; for it cannot be that a prophet perish out of Jerusalem. The story of the last fatal visit to Jerusalem, the accomplishment of the purpose of the Jews to destroy him, we must leave to a subsequent chapter; but it completes the evidence against Jerusalem. And even after the death of Jesus the Jews altered neither in spirit nor conduct. Paul wrote to the Thessalonians: "For ye, brethren, became imitators of the churches of God (i.e. the Christians) which are in Judæa in Christ Jesus; for ye also suffered the same things of your own country-men as they did of the Jews, who both killed the Lord Jesus and the prophets, and drove us out, and please not God, and are contrary to all men, forbidding us to speak to the Gentiles, that they may be saved."

More than ever it seems to grow clear that Christianity owes nothing to Judaism. The sweet and pure and universal religion of Jesus was entirely foreign to the thought of the Jews; it was an original growth, but it unfolded itself in his heart in Galilee and not in Judæa.

V.

JESUS AND THE GENTILES.

———◦———

In the previous chapters I have tried to show how Jesus regarded everything essentially Jewish with dislike, and treated it with the freest and most independent criticism. The holy city, Jerusalem, had no charms for him; the Law of Moses seemed to him only an imperfect code suited to early times, which was superseded by the higher spiritual and moral consciousness which he personally, with some of Israel's greatest prophets, had attained. The traditions and precepts of the Scribes and Pharisees he regarded with undisguised contempt, and the personal character of the leading classes of the Jews provoked his warm indignation.

Important light is thrown upon the character and disposition of Jesus by another and entirely different set of circumstances, which may generally be described as his conduct towards the Gentiles. This was always marked by sympathy, patience, kindness and hopefulness—a marked contrast to his attitude towards the Jews, and a marked contrast also to the behaviour of

the strict Jews to the Gentiles. In matters of busi-
ness, no doubt, they were sometimes compelled to
have dealings with them, though they avoided them
as much as possible ; but this did not incline them to
friendliness or personal intercourse. Even the disciples
are said to have wondered that he conversed with the
woman at Sychar, for the Jews had no dealings with
the Samaritans.

This disposition of Jesus was almost incomprehensible to the writers of the Synoptic Gospels, whose
sympathies were Jewish, but whose candour prevented
them suppressing many things that told against the
race. And so with regard to the Gentiles, the Evangelists did not understand all that was implied either
by the words or deeds of Jesus. They could not
altogether conceal the fact of his extraordinary pre-
ference for the Gentiles, though they tried to lessen
its significance.

There are some reported sayings which are adverse
to the Gentiles, and might be alleged against the
statement just made. But the general tendency is as
I have stated. There are more and severer things
said against the Jews than against the Gentiles. If
Jesus said, " In praying, use not vain repetitions as
the Gentiles do," he also said that the Scribes and
Pharisees "for a pretence made long prayers." If he
said that the Gentiles sought after the things of the

world, the Evangelist was also obliged to admit that the Pharisees were lovers of money.

In the first three Gospels we learn that the ministry of Jesus commenced, and was pursued principally, amongst the mixed population of Galilee or in the Decapolis, the neighbourhood of Tyre and Sidon and Cæsarea Philippi. The cities where most of his mighty works were done were on the borders of the lake—Capernaum, Bethsaida and Chorazin. It was of a Gentile he said, " I have not found so great faith in Israel." To the Jews he said, " Many shall come from the east and the west, and sit down with Abraham and Isaac and Jacob in the kingdom of heaven, but the children of the kingdom shall be cast into outer darkness."

If there were any Israelites he cared about, it was not the orthodox Jews, but the latitudinarian or apostates who had come under Gentile influence. If he told a story, it was to the advantage of the Gentiles or Samaritans. Such especially is the parable of the Good Samaritan. It does not teach the duty of tolerance towards unbelievers, or that a Samaritan was as good as a Jew, but that he was a great deal better ; that the priests and the levites, with their formal religion and unimpeachable orthodoxy, had less true religion than the outsider whose religion was more natural and more humane. He is said on one occasion to have spoken words of kindness, if not of actual healing, to ten lepers; but only one of them returned to give thanks to God, and he was a Samaritan. In the parable of the Servants, it is the Jews, who knew their Lord's will and did it not, who are most severely condemned; a much milder sentence is passed upon the unconscious Gentiles.

The prodigal son returning contrite and penitent to his father is a picture of the Gentiles, while the harsh and selfish elder brother is a picture of the Jews.

There is one story in which the regard of Jesus for the Gentiles is most distinctly and emphatically expressed, and the bearing of his utterances was fully understood by the Jews, whom it aroused into a paroxysm of anger. It is the story of his preaching in the synagogue of his city, Nazareth. It might be thought that this incident tells very forcibly against the general view exhibited in these pages; that it is contradictory of the opinion that the Galileans were more tolerant and liberal than the Jews of the south The exceptional character of the incident, however, does not destroy the general impression. We can only suppose that the persons who attended the synagogue at Nazareth on the occasion, and who approached in their thoughts and habits the temper of the Judæans, were only a small part of the population. No doubt there were such groups scattered about Galilee, but they were the exception and not the rule. According to Luke, Jesus had already become popular in the neighbouring country, and one Sabbath he entered the synagogue of his native town. During the service he stood up, to signify his wish to read. And he read from Isaiah : " The spirit of the Lord is upon me," &c.; and when he had finished the reading, he addressed them in his own words. And they all wondered at the gracious words he uttered. "And they said, Is not this the son of Joseph ? And he said, Doubtless ye will say unto me, Physician, heal thyself. Whatsoever we have heard that you have done in Capernaum, do here also in your own country. And he said, No prophet is acceptable in his own country. There were many widows in Israel in the days of Elijah, but unto none of them was he sent, but only to Sarepta in the land of Sidon, unto a woman that was a widow. And there were many lepers in Israel in the time of Elisha, and none of them was cleansed, only Naaman the Syrian." The significance of these allusions was too plain to be mistaken. It was that the Gentiles were more ready to receive the prophets of God than the Jews themselves, and that he had found a readier welcome himself among strangers than the people of his own town·would give him. They were all filled with wrath as they heard these things, and rose up and hustled him out of the place. They could not bear to be told that their haughty assumption of being the chosen and favoured people of God had no foundation, but was only a dream of their own pride and exclusiveness.

It is this un-Jewish cast of mind which explains the things Jesus did, which the Pharisees could not understand. He observed no fasts; he came eating and drinking, and they called him a wine-bibber and a glutton. He excited their wrath by his neglect of the rigid observance of the Sabbath. He and his disciples ate with unwashen hands. This is a particular mark of his indifference to Jewish tradition, as Mark says: "For the Pharisees *and all the Jews*, except they wash their hands diligently, eat not." He had intimate and friendly intercourse with tax-gatherers and apostates. At heart he was more of a Gentile than a Jew; and once this came home so forcibly to some of the Jews, that they gave vent to their feelings in the words, "Thou art a Samaritan."

The fact seems undeniable that, in his intercourse with the Gentiles and the Jews, Jesus found that the Gentiles were more receptive of his teaching than the Jews, and, in the phraseology of the time, were nearer the kingdom of heaven. The conservative self-satisfaction of the Jews was the great obstacle to their reformation. They were sunken below the Gentiles in their incapacity to receive the truth. They were so bound by their ancient laws and traditions and customs that they were incapable of improvement;

while the Gentiles were open-minded, receptive, eager to learn and ready to reform.

When the Jews came seeking a miraculous sign from him, he said : "A wicked and adulterous generation asks for a sign ; but no sign shall be given it, except the sign of the prophet Jonah. On the day of judgment the men of Nineveh shall stand beside this generation and condemn, for *they* repented at the preaching of Jonah, and behold, a greater than Jonah is here." By which he implied that the heathen Ninevites repented at the preaching of Jonah, but that the Jews would not repent at the preaching of a prophet of their own day.

One thing is clear from the tendency of all these instances of the friendliness of Jesus to the Gentiles, whom the Jews avoided and hated, and that is, that he had learned to look upon every man as a brother, and would not allow differences of race or creed to limit his goodwill.   It is also clear that this spirit was not derived from Judaism, and that even if Jesus were a Jew by birth, he was not a Jew by nature or in disposition.

VI.

JESUS IN GALILEE.

———◦———

WE have thus far been brought face to face with a very interesting and important question. We have seen that Jesus did not consider himself bound by the traditions of the Rabbis, nor even by the Law of Moses ; that the Jews were regarded by him as the hypocritical and superstitious upholders of a formal religion ; that Jerusalem had no attractions for him, and was to his mind the focus of bigotry and persecution. Christianity never took root amongst the Jews; they are unconverted to this day. It did take root amongst the Gentiles ; and it is the descendants of the pagans, and not of the Israelites, who compose the Christian world. The question therefore is, Who and what was this Teacher from Nazareth who did not convert the Jews, but who did convert the pagans ? Was he, as it is so often said, the product of centuries of Judaism ? Was it for him that the race had been chosen ? Was Judaism really the preparation for Christianity ? If so, why have not the Jews themselves recognized it, and why has not Christianity abolished Judaism? It looks almost as if, though appearing amongst the Jews, Jesus was not a Jew himself. But was he a Gentile? This hardly seems likely, or he would not have interested himself in the Jews as much as he did, or have shown himself so well acquainted with their system. What was he, then? He was something of a Jew and something of a Gentile, yet better than either of them.

The first thing necessary is to fix our attention upon the place where he was born and educated, and where his mind developed. He was not born in Jerusalem, nor anywhere in Judæa, but in Nazareth, a town of Galilee. He was not a Judæan, but a Galilean; and it is here we shall find the explanation we want.

We often think and speak of Palestine in the time of Jesus as if it were a united country or kingdom; but this it had not been for centuries. Under Solomon and David it had been, but subsequently it was divided into the two kingdoms of Judah and Israel; and though it was no longer a kingdom, the divisions survived. The two tribes of Judah and Benjamin, with Dan and Simeon, composed the southern population; and the other tribes, the northern. The part that was afterwards known as Galilee was the portion of the countries originally allotted to Issachar, Zebulon, Asher and Naphtali; the country between Galilee and Judæa being known as Samaria. In the time of Jesus the separation of the provinces was very distinct. A Roman, Pontius Pilate, governed Judæa ; an Idumæan, Herod, governed Galilee. In the New Testament we do not read of Palestine, but of Judæa, Samaria, Galilee, &c. Galilee and Judæa are recognized as being absolutely distinct from each other. They were not very far apart, Nazareth being only seventy miles or so from Jerusalem. Though the distance was not great, the characteristics of the country and of the people differed considerably. Judæa, especially in the neighbourhood of Jerusalem, was, on the whole, a barren, rugged, mountainous country. The Jews were very exclusive, and had very little toleration for the Gentiles. Especially at Jerusalem, which was a city of priests, they were engrossed in their own religion, learning, customs and law. They were, with all their pride of race, narrow and bigoted, and, with all their affectation of learning, ignorant of the world.

Galilee was a very different district. In the first place, it was the most beautiful part of Syria ; though hilly, it was not so mountainous as Judæa. The south part was the celebrated plain of Jezreel, or Esdraelon, as it was called by the Greeks—one vast corn-field, many miles in extent. The hills of Naphtali are of jagged outline and varied vegetation, presenting a striking contrast to the monotonous scenery of Judæa. From Tabor to Nazareth, the scenery resembled that of an English park, with its mixture of greensward and woodland. Van de Velde said, describing the view from Lebanon : " I have travelled in no part of the world where I have seen such a variety of glorious mountain scenes within so narrow a compass. Here, in one word, you find all that the eye could desire to behold on this earth. The whole of northern Canaan lies at our feet." And it was a similar scene which Mohammed beheld from Damascus, which made him sigh—" Man has but one Paradise, and mine is fixed elsewhere." Northern Canaan was the land described by the author of the Book of Deuteronomy, a description totally inapplicable to the south : " A land of brooks and water, of fountains and depths springing forth in valleys and hills ; a land of wheat and barley, and vines and fig-trees and pomegranates ; a land of oil, olive and honey ; a land where thou shalt eat bread without scarceness." It was indeed a beautiful land, a land of trees and fields and flowers and birds. It was rightly likened to a Paradise. Josephus, in a well-known passage, calls it an ambitious effort of Nature ; for from the low-lying plain of Gennesareth by the lake of that name, with its almost tropical climate, to the higher ground in the interior, every variety of temperature might be found, suitable for an unexampled variety of vegetation in so limited a space. The plain of Gennesareth by the lake was called the Garden of the East ; the lake itself presenting so striking a contrast to the lake of

Judæa, the Salt or Dead Sea, that Dean Stanley called the Lake of Galilee a Sea of Life.

The lake itself was no retired mountain tarn, solitary and desolate, but a scene of busy and brilliant activity. No less than ten important towns stood upon its borders, and hundreds of fishermen followed their calling upon its surface ; and when we add, says Stanley, "the crowd of ship-builders, the many boats of traffic, pleasure and passage, we see that the whole basin must have been a focus of life and energy. The surface of the lake constantly dotted over with the white sails of vessels, flying before the mountain gusts, as the beach sparkled with the houses and palaces, the synagogues and temples of the Jewish and Roman inhabitants."—"I have created seven seas, saith the Lord, but out of them I have chosen none but the Sea of Gennesareth," was a Rabbinical way of expressing the native appreciation of the locality.

It follows, as a matter of course, we might say, that such a beautiful and productive country was at that time populous and wealthy. Josephus, who was the military governor of Galilee, ought to have known what the facts were ; but his statements are generally doubted and often denied. It is certainly probable that his account is somewhat exaggerated, but it is not likely it was without foundation. He says that there were in Galilee no less than two hundred and four towns and villages, the smallest of which had

fifteen thousand inhabitants. If something considerably less than this were true, as very likely it was
(Renan reduces the last figure to five thousand), it
must still have been a busy and wealthy district. To
speak of Galilee, as writers often do, as poor, obscure
and despised, is nothing less than preposterous. Reading Josephus' history of the war in Galilee, we are made
to feel that we are in the midst of an active, important
and thriving country. There were many fortified
cities, and Sepphoris, which was the Roman capital
of the district before the city of Tiberias was built by
the lake-side, was only six miles from Nazareth itself.
Rabbi Jose, who lived in Galilee, said, "For sixteen
miles on either side of Sepphoris there flows milk and
honey."

Nazareth is called a town, and not a village, so that
it was a place of some importance, and it was in a
most beautiful situation. It was surrounded by hills
in a rich and lovely field. An old writer said: "It
was a rose, and, like a rose, enclosed by mountains as
the flower by leaves." It was in this pretty and prosperous town, and not in a miserable and obscure
village, that Jesus was born, and in its beautiful seclu-
sion he passed his youth. Yet after giving a description of the place, which agrees with the above, Dean
Stanley speaks of its wild character, high up among
the Galilean hills. As a matter of fact, it is only
about half as high as Jerusalem, and the hills are

incomparably gentler and more beautiful than those
of Judæa, of which Lady Strangford said : "The hill
scenery, viewed from the Mount of Olives, is the
dreariest, barrenest, ugliest, to be seen anywhere."

But what was the condition of the people of Galilee?
That they were prosperous there can be no doubt ; a
fertile country, a large population, busy cities, active
commerce and manufactures, all denote prosperity.
And under Herod Antipas they were quiet and peaceful, while the Jews of the south were always in trouble
with the Roman soldiers. The population of Galilee
was a mixed one : there were more Gentiles there
than Jews. Romans, Greeks, Syrians, Phœnicians,
mingled together in the principal cities ; and naturally
this had an influence over those whom, for the want
of a better name, we call Jews. They lived on friendly
terms. One of the Gentile rulers had built them a
synagogue. The natural consequence of this intercourse was, that they were more liberal-minded, less
bigoted, than the Judæans. Though it was said that
the Galileans were zealous for the law, and the Jews
were zealous for money, it must not be inferred that
it was the Levitical law which commanded the zeal of
the Galileans. Judaism, which grew up after the return
from the exile, was concentrated in Jerusalem ; the religion of the Galileans was rather that of Deuteronomy,
of Isaiah and Jeremiah. The Galileans themselves
were probably descended from the ancient four tribes,

who had always kept themselves separate from the inhabitants of the south; and not unlikely, like the Samaritans, had mixed by marriage with the other inhabitants, who had not all been driven out at the conquest. They were not over-awed, as were the Judæans, by the presence of the temple and a host of priests. Their worship was only that of the synagogue, where prayers were said, the Law and the prophets read, addresses delivered, discussions held, and education given. We notice the freedom of the synagogue many times in the New Testament. Questions were asked and answered; disputes waxed warm within the walls at what we should call service-time. All these things tended to make the Galileans broad-minded and free-thinking—all the more as they mingled with people of other races and religions. The Jews of Jerusalem may have despised the Galileans, though the evidence for it is only slight—much as the narrow-minded and exclusive inhabitants of a cathedral city may despise the people in the manufacturing towns, or as an Oxford man may look down upon a Londoner; but in such cases the contempt is generally returned with interest; it does not follow that the class which considers itself the superior one is so in fact. And we see that the Galilean treated the Pharisees and priests with the contempt they deserved. The character of Jesus was no doubt largely formed by his environment and associations.

Where nature is niggardly, man becomes covetous; so the southern Jews were lovers of money. But where nature is prodigal, man is careless; it was the Galilean, impressed by the bounty of God in nature around him, exclaimed, "Be not anxious for the morrow."

There is another curious thing which may throw some light upon the personality of Jesus. Archdeacon Farrar has noticed that none of the portraits of Jesus ever represent him as a Jew. His features are paler and of a more Grecian type, more like those of a descendant of the people who were living in the land before the Israelitish settlement. This physical unlikeness to the Jews may explain the charge, if we may consider it one, once made by the Pharisees against Jesus—"Thou art a Samaritan." Dean Stanley says the Samaritans were distinguished by their noble physiognomy and stately appearance from all other branches of the children of Israel. So Jesus may have resembled the Samaritans more than he did the Jews.

Jesus may have received his religion at first from the Galilean Israelites; but even then it was purer and broader than that of Jerusalem; and he had further come under two great influences which had tended to modify it still more. The first was that of his Gentile neighbours; amongst them he gave up the idea that the old Israelitish religion was the only

one and the true. He learned to feel that God cared
for all men, that His sun shone and His rain fell with
a blessed impartiality on all alike. He saw Jews and
Greeks and Romans and Syrians all living much the
same kind of life—some worshipping in synagogues
and some in temples—but all moved by the same
impulses and desires. He saw them all alike toiling
and wearying, sinning and suffering, sorrowing and
dying. He saw that the Gentiles feared God, loved
their families, cared for their neighbours; and so he
lost faith in Judaism, and placed his faith in his
Heavenly Father and in humanity. His sympathies
were even more with the Gentiles than with the
Jews; and as his faith widened and his love deepened,
he became less and less of an Israelite, and yet not a
Gentile, but only more perfectly a man.

VII.

JESUS AND NATURE.

I HAVE already said that there can be no doubt that Jesus felt very deeply the influence of the beautiful natural scenery amidst which his life was for the most part spent. Before he came forward as a public teacher, he had lived for thirty years in the districts of Zebulon and Naphtali, not only the most beautiful part of Palestine, but among the loveliest places of the East. Here, in the intervals of work and on the Sabbath-days, he roamed over the green hills and amongst the corn-fields, and sometimes visited the Sea of Galilee and enjoyed the scenes in the romantic Garden of Gennesareth. He watched the clouds and the sky; noted how, when the sky was red, it betokened fine weather, and when it was lowering he saw signs of rain. Nothing escaped his eye. He watched the birds of the air and the flowers of the field; he pondered on the mysterious growth of seeds; and the reeds shaken by the wind arrested his glance. All these things, and many more, he treasured in his mind, and afterwards drew upon the stores of his memory for the illustration of his teaching.

Galilee was indeed a beautiful district, stretching from the plain of Esdraelon to the feet of Lebanon, and from the Lake of Galilee to the great sea. Travellers looking over it from the hills have declared it to be one of the fairest scenes on earth. Mohammed, gazing longingly over it from Damascus, regretted that he could not remain there for ever. "If nature could influence mind, if it could create genius, Naphtali would be a land of poets." Most, if not all, the Hebrew prophets came from the north. It was from Kadesh Naphtali that Barak, who sang the song of triumph with Deborah, came. The Song of Songs, so full of nature-pictures, was inspired in the same locality. Many of the Psalms contain indications of the same local origin. "The north and the south, thou hast created them. Tabor and Hermon shall rejoice in thy name."

"In a spot like Nazareth," says Keim, "it is impossible to imagine a people spiritually destitute if nature has a word to say in the development of man." "If nature could influence mind"? "If nature has a word to say in the development of man"? Surely there is no influence so potent.

> For in the open halls of space,
> The Truth floats free upon the wind ;
> We speak with Wisdom face to face,
> And Love infects the docile mind.

We generally only think of Jesus referring to nature

for illustrations of his parables. But these numerous references are the signs of a long and close and affectionate familiarity with nature. The details were idealized by a religious imagination. Behold the lilies of the field! Galilee was a land of flowers; oleanders grew by the lake-side, gay tulips and anemones bespangled the fields and hills. The land glowed with flowers, and was arrayed in beauty with which the glory of kings could not compare, in the estimation of the poet. Behold the birds of the air! The lake-country was a land of birds. The corn grew freely up to the very edge of the road-side, and the scattered seed fell among thorns or on the stony ground, and it did not escape his notice. In the summer-time he saw all about him the fields white unto harvest, so plenteous that the labourers seemed too few. He saw sometimes the tares growing in the midst of the wheat, and the husbandmen leaving them until the ingathering. He saw the good trees bringing forth good fruit, and the tiny mustard-seed, in that favourable climate, growing into one of the largest of bushes, so that the birds could lodge in its branches. All these and a thousand more things he saw and treasured in his memory.

We think of these illustrations of his parables as disconnected references to details which here and there might catch the observant eye. We forget the mind and the imagination which were behind the

eye. Those who spend much time in beautiful scenes,
if their minds are cultivated and their spirits pure,
acquire a great deal more than a mere acquaintance
with details. The scenes are photographed upon the
brain, and remain a permanent source of delight.
They come back to us unbidden, and refresh us when
we are far away. One view of nature, or even an
occasional one, does not make this impression. It
takes many a loving hour to drink in all the influences
nature is capable of imparting. We have to lose our-
selves in it, and let its spirit sink into hearts. So we
think Jesus must have done.

> "What soul was his, when, from the naked top
> Of some bold headland, he beheld the sun
> Rise up, and bathe the world in light ! He looked—
> Ocean and earth, the solid frame of earth
> And ocean's liquid mass, before him lay
> In gladness and deep joy. The clouds were touched,
> And in their silent faces did he read
> Unutterable love. Sound needed none,
> Nor any voice of joy; his spirit drank
> The spectacle ; sensation, soul, and form
> All melted into him ; they swallowed up
> His animal being ; in them did he live,
> And by them did he live ; they were his life.
> In such access of mind, in such high hour
> Of visitation from the living God,
> Thought was not ; in enjoyment it expired.
> No thanks he breathed, he proffered no request.
> Rapt into still communion that transcends
> The imperfect offices of prayer and praise,
> His mind was a thanksgiving to the Power
> That made him ; it was blessedness and love !"*

* The Excursion, Book i.

This description, borrowed from Wordsworth, may seem too poetical to apply to Jesus. I do not think it is. Nature, to Jesus, was in the highest sense religious. He was at heart a poet; but so strong was the religious idea within him, that in the main it overpowered the poetic feeling. But the poetic feeling on its side helped to mould the religious idea. As he watched the birds, he reflected that God fed them; if he admired the flowers, it was God who clothed them; and he thought how much happier men would be if they could trust God with the unbounded trust of birds and the careless faith of flowers.

In this way, too, he learned from the impartial prodigality of nature to believe in the unlimited benevolence of God, and discarded the narrow sentiments of the "chosen" people. Why should we only love those that love us, and do good to those that do good to us? As he watched the sun rising over the distant hills, he saw its beams fall on good and evil alike, and the fertilizing rain fell on the fields and gardens of Gentile and Israelite without distinction. Why should not man be as generous as God?

And in this light he saw in their true perspective the ancient law and the modern traditions, and realized that true religion was to "love God above all things earthly, and every man as a brother." The religion of ritual and ceremony seemed contemptible beside this. Communion with nature, where it is soft and

beautiful, softens and makes gentle the heart of man ;
it lifts him above the pettiness of social differences
and religious divisions, and nourishes in the soul an
all-embracing charity. The root of love is gentleness;
and nowhere is gentleness so perfectly fostered as in
the fair solitudes of the fields and hills. Descending
from them into the busy haunts of men, Jesus looked
upon his fellows with a new emotion, with a perfect
sympathy and a yearning love. As he saw them
weary under the burdens of life, and uncomforted
under the yoke of a formal religion, he cried : " Come
unto me, all ye that are heavy-laden, and I will give
you rest. Take my yoke upon you and learn of me ;
for my yoke is easy and my burden is light."

To understand religion, we need the broad view
which is only to be found by sympathy with nature
and a wide intercourse with our fellow-men. We do
not find it in the dusty records of the past, in the dry
disquisitions of scholastic theologians, in the dreary
controversies of narrow-minded doctrinaires. We study
the writings of men of other days, their systems and
creeds ; they interest us, but they do not give us life,
nor rest, nor love. Religion comes to us in quite
another way. And so it was in the case of Jesus.
The Pharisees might be particular about their dress
and their fasts and their washings. The Scribes might
discuss the meaning of ancient laws and words, the
proper interpretation of this sentence or the true

importance of that; the priests might offer their sacrifices of fire and blood in the gorgeous temple; but
what could all this do for the weary-burdened souls
of men?

So the message Jesus brought with him from the
fields and the hills seemed to bring new life and happiness to those who heard it. He talked, not of Moses,
as did the Scribes, but of a Heavenly Father ever
ready to give His good Spirit to those who asked it;
who desired mercy and not sacrifice, purity of heart
and not the washing of hands. And in place of a
thousand commands, he gave them two, which needed
no Scribe to expound, and which the poorest of his
hearers could fulfil.

He made the people feel that happiness could be
found only in heartfelt love to the celestial Father,
and that all the irksome precepts of the Law could be
dispensed with if they would love one another. And
this was the Gospel which came out of Galilee.

VIII

THE TEACHER.

———•+•+•———

I HAVE been gradually trying to draw a picture of what I take to be the real Jesus, the Galilean who founded Christianity. Very briefly I have traced some of the points in his career which enable us to form an opinion of his character. We have noticed how he regarded the Law, the various ceremonies of the Jews, and the traditions of the Pharisees. We have seen how unfriendly he was to the Jews themselves, and how patient and friendly he was to the Gentiles. I might almost say we have discovered that Galilee, and not Jerusalem, is the proper place to study his life. In Galilee, he was at home amongst friends ; in Judæa, he was amongst foes.

I have passed by the stories relating his alleged miraculous birth at Bethlehem, and have taken it for granted that he was the son of Joseph and Mary of Nazareth. The two different stories of the incarnation in Matthew and Luke are quite unhistoric, and cannot be made to agree ; they are never again referred to even in those Gospels, and are not mentioned by

Mark and John; they are never noticed by Paul or any other of the New Testament writers, as they must have been had they been true.

The story of the dark days which came upon him towards the end of his brief career, the clouds that darkened the afternoon which followed the morning sunshine, is much more important than the legends of his birth. How did it come about that so beautiful an idyll as the early life of the Galilean should so suddenly deepen into the darkness of the tragedy of Calvary?

We have already seen how the quarrel with the Jews began, and it is not difficult to follow the development of it; how dislike deepened into hatred, and hatred begot treachery and falsehood; and how, since he could not be silenced, he was doomed to fall a victim to Pharaisaic pride and priestly anger. And then we see how the serene religion he had learned amongst the Galilean hills stood by him in the council-chamber of the judge and comforted him on the cross. All this, and much more, it is not difficult to discern when we once learn to appreciate his real character. And we find, too, he was no Jewish Messiah nor ecclesiastical Christ, but one of the gentlest and humblest and least pretending of the sons of men.

We sometimes speak of Jesus as a prophet, yet this is not strictly correct. He is so called on one occasion—"This is Jesus, the prophet of Nazareth;" but this was a popular use of the expression, meaning only a teacher of unusual influence.   The ancient prophets were of a different type, of which John was more a representative than Jesus.   They denounced the sins of the nation, predicted calamities or anticipated triumphs.   They were men who stood alone—who sometimes seem to walk across the stage, utter their stern message, and disappear.   They had no followers ; they left no school behind them ; they founded no religion.   They delivered their warning or their word of cheer, and were seen no more.

There was more of the poet than the prophet about Jesus ; at first, at least, he spoke with a serene impersonality about God and life and nature.   He did not threaten or condemn.   His messages fell as gentle as the sunshine, as refreshing as the rain.   We may well ask, How was it possible for a man who did so little to accomplish so much ?   It was because he was an original soul—one who did not borrow his thoughts and his religion from the past, but derived them at first-hand from God, his soul and nature.

His God was not the God of the Jews—not the God of the Law, or the temple, or the Pharisees.   They had caught no glimpse of the Heavenly Father.   Their religion was in some respects a high one ; at least at its centre was the belief in one God and a detestation of idolatry.   But it had never converted the world. It was taught in a way, and associated with rites and ceremonies, that had no attraction for the Greek or Roman. It remained the religion of the Jews alone, and it has done so to this day.

The religion of Jesus was original. His God was not the God of the Jews alone, but of the Gentiles also. The service he required was such as every soul could render in purity of heart, in loveliness of life, in the spirituality of divine communion. He was not a prophet, but a teacher—one who was fully in sympathy with every phase of life, and able to impart his message to men of every rank and creed. It was of universal import, and was only rejected by the Jews because they were so case-hardened in their ancestral beliefs that they would listen to nothing that conflicted with them. It was joyfully received by the pagans, because they were weary with their ineffectual search after God, which happily they felt to have been ineffectual, and so they were ready to welcome new and inspiriting truth.

This account of the character of Jesus may appear to many to be correct from a certain point of view. It is not difficult to realize the personality of the Teacher who succeeded in impressing his listeners with new and beautiful thoughts about the Fatherhood of God and the simple religious life which would bring men near to Him. There is a simplicity and natural-ness about the picture which bear the stamp of truth ; but yet I own it may be objected that it is not alto-

gether the Jesus we read about in the Gospels. It is
true as far as it goes, but is it all the truth? There
is another part of the picture which I have not touched,
and which I should be glad to leave alone if I could.
But I shall be asked, What about the stories of Jesus
healing the sick, casting-out demons, raising the dead,
turning the water into wine, stilling the tempest, and
the rest? I think some of these stories may be
founded upon some fact ; that some are due to exaggeration ; and some due to later invention, growing
out of the tendency of the early Christians, like that
of so many other people, to believe in marvels, and to
attribute miracles to the Founder of their religion.
The stories of Jesus raising the dead, I have no hesita-
tion in saying, I think altogether unfounded. No
man ever raised the dead. Unfounded also are those
stories which attributed to him any power over Nature.
Natural forces obey natural laws, and must for ever
be insensible to the influence of the human will or
human words.

The other two classes of miracles need not be dis-
posed of so summarily. I mean the stories of healing
and the casting-out of demons. These may be in
part true, in part exaggeration, and in part erroneous
presentation.

First, as to healing. No doubt this is greatly exaggerated ; that is, as to the kinds of diseases healed and
the number of people cured. In some places it is

said that the people of certain districts brought all
their sick to him, and he healed them all. This might
have grown up out of the fact that he had exerted an
influence for good over the health of a few. I think
there can be no doubt that it is possible in some cases,
perhaps of peculiar disorders, a man can exert such
an influence over others as to do them good physically,
and drive away nervous and perhaps other diseases.
The belief in this kind of healing is so general that it
is probably founded on occasional instances. All the
world over, especially in the East, belief in occult
healing prevails. No doubt many people profess to
effect the "mind-cure" who are mere pretenders, but
others have the power. There is a great deal of
mystery yet about the relations of mind and body ;
but it is hardly disputed in these days that their influence is reciprocal ; and while a disordered physical
condition will affect the reason and the affections, a
favourable emotion will in many cases restore the
health. It is not supernatural ; it is only a neglected
branch of therapeutics. Jesus may have wrought
some cures in this way, though he may not have
understood how it came about, except that he possessed the power. Those who believed in him trusted
him ; and when he said, " Be healed," their own minds
wrought the cure. We know very well that if a man
were successful in a few cases of this kind, his powers
would soon be exaggerated by the imagination of

those at a distance, or of those who heard the stories after he was dead.

The accounts of the curing of demoniacs may be explained in the same way. I do not believe in the existence of demons, still less in their power to enter into men and women. But the thing has a sort of reality to those who do believe it. This and similar beliefs have always been common amongst superstitious people. Madness, epilepsy, convulsions, have been ascribed to demoniacal possession. The well-known story in Josephus is sufficient evidence of the existence of the belief amongst the Jews—"and this kind of healing to this day is very usual among those of our nation," is conclusive of the prevalence of exorcism during the first century. As to those in the Gospels who were said to have been possessed, they no doubt were the subjects of temporary aberration. The Jews thought that a madman was possessed ; as they said of Jesus, " He hath a demon and is mad." The two things were the same in their minds ; and of another, of whom a devil was said to have been cast out, it was afterwards declared that he was in his right mind.

These kind of mental disorders are not uncommon. They are often, doubtless, not real madness, but delusions. Men thought they were possessed, and acted as if they were. If a man believed that a demon was in him, he would give up all self-control and believe the demon made him do what he liked. The remark of Josephus proves that this kind of disorder was common in Syria. It was all an illusion, doubtless ; but to a man who is subject to an illusion, the illusion is a reality. And these illusions are contagious ; if one man is excited by them, others contract the same disorder. There are numberless instances of it ; whole districts have been at times afflicted with the same mania.

But what could Jesus have had to do with disorders of this kind ? If he had anything to do with them, it would probably have been in this way : that now and then he may have been brought into contact with a poor man or child suffering from this semi-lunacy, or hysteria, or epilepsy, and something in his presence, or even in his reputation, would produce such an impression as to effect a cure. His self-control, his serene self-possession, his softening look, or his decisive voice, might have driven away, not the demon, but the disorder. This is certainly possible, but it must be distinguished from the superstition of the times.

F

IX.

THE LAST JOURNEY.

THE life of Jesus as we know it, understanding by
it so much as was spent publicly, can be reckoned by
months; at the most, only two or three years could
have elapsed from the day he listened to the preaching
of John the Baptist on the banks of Jordan, till the
fatal hour when he trod the path that led to Calvary.
During the interval most of the time had been spent
in the country. When he had listened to John preaching the coming of the kingdom of God, and had felt
himself moved by an impulse and an inspiration to
turn preacher and teacher as well, it was not to Jerusalem he went. He may have visited the city, have
looked upon its busy throngs, have seen the temple
and the priests, the lawyers and the soldiers; but
there was nothing in all this with which the gentle
religious man could sympathize. He was used to the
peaceful solitudes of the country; to thoughts of God
as he wandered in the fields or by the shores of the
lake; to the simple religious services of the village synagogue; to converse with his friends, who knew nothing

of the busy political and ecclesiastical world of Jerusalem. For him to go to Jerusalem would be something like a village Dissenter going up to some large city and visiting the Catholic cathedral, where everything might seem very grand, but would at the same time impress him less favourably than his beloved village chapel.

But the time came when he felt that he must go up to Jerusalem—that he must speak in the larger world to be found there—must, if necessary, try his strength against the powerful and learned men of the day, or else give up his mission altogether. So he started on this last pilgrimage, from which he had an early presentiment that he would never return.

He left his native country never to see it again. It seems very hard that such must have been the case, that it was not possible for him to remain quietly at home, speaking lessons of truth and beauty to his friends and disciples as they strolled together through the fields or sat together on the hill-sides. He must have turned many a loving farewell glance upon the dear familiar scenes as he set his face to go to Jerusalem. There was the old home where he had worked side by side with his father the carpenter; he saw the fields and the flowers and the lake, and remembered all the peaceful days of his youth, and the holy visions and hopes that had been his. He bade them all good-bye; the pleasant days had passed away; he must now traverse, step by step, the thorny path that will terminate only in the anguish of death.

At first, probably, he had no foreboding. He was only going to deliver his message to a wider world, to proclaim the kingdom of God near the very courts of the temple ; and the young preacher and lover of truth always at first believes that, if he can only be heard, men will gladly receive his message. He has nothing but the truth, which to him seems so beautiful, to proclaim. How can men reject it? He does not want to upset religion ; he only desires to tell men how to make their religion more perfect and acceptable to God.

So he went his way. He was surrounded, we are told, not only by his little circle of friends, but by a more considerable band of followers, probably drawn for the most part from the cities by the lake, going up to Jerusalem on their own account, but in his company. There were not very many of them altogether, but they were gay and cheerful and full of bright anticipations. We have already seen how he was received in Jerusalem, and need not repeat the description of the visit. On one side was the temple, the priesthood, and all the organized religion of Judæa ; and on the other was the simple, pure-hearted Galilean Teacher and his humble friends.

It is marvellous how at times the sweet and effortless productions of unpretending affection and nature excel the efforts of art. The unambitious writers of the Gospel narratives equal in their unstrained effects the works of the greatest masters. Nowhere in literature is there anything that surpasses in skill the telling of the story of the last few days of the life of Jesus. There is the greatest dramatic effect of vivid contrast, of telling dialogue, of heroic veracity and scheming duplicity. Passion and pathos, gentle friendship and bitter intriguing hate, are brought face to face and condensed in the touching record of the events which did not take a week to accomplish, and which terminated with the tragedy of Calvary. As Jesus drew near the city, he was unable to repress the demonstrations of love and popularity which greeted him. As their chosen leader, riding on an ass, his friends walking beside him, he entered the city amidst the greetings of those who waited for him. The elders waved green boughs, and the children ran before and shouted. When the strangers in the city, wondering at the lively scene, asked, "Who is this?" the bystanders replied, "This is Jesus, the Prophet of Nazareth." Before the next Sabbath sun arose, that bright life was extinguished—the Prophet had met a martyr's fate. Swift, but not altogether unexpected, was the work of hate, but still more unexpected was the immortality of truth and love. The Galilean was crucified, but the religion of the Cross was born. It was not unexpected: a few days before, when the country people began to journey towards Jerusalem, there was curious questioning in the city as to whether Jesus would come; for it was already known that the chief-priests and Pharisees had issued orders that if any man knew where he was, he should show it that they might take him. While many loved, more already hated, him, and had planned his doom. By the time Jesus reached the city, he had probably realized what the end would be; but he would not flee like a coward from the consequences of his own words. And it may be, as it is related, that his insight, quickened by the impending conflict, gave him to see that, so far from his death being a defeat, it would give a new and commanding authority to the words he had spoken, and a lasting influence to the life he had led. He had then no share in the rejoicing of the multitude, as he saw in one broad generalization the utter depravity of the priests and people, and the ensigns of the con-queror over all; he knew the greatness and glory of Jerusalem had departed for ever. In the parable of the Barren Fig-tree, he described the utter blight and sterility which had fallen upon Judaism, and he fore-told the coming desolation which no one saw but he; and his heart forgot its own sorrows as he remembered the sins and foresaw the sufferings of the descendants of Israel. At first it seemed to his enemies that their plans would be defeated; his popularity was more than they had counted upon. "See," said they, "the whole city is gone after him; and they feared the people." Intriguing with a treacherous follower, they found where he spent his unprotected nights far away from the friendly crowd; there they resolved to fall upon him. The contest was soon over. He understood what was destined for him. He used the last opportunity given him for speaking from his heart, no longer in winning and persuasive words, but in fulfilling the stern duty of a messenger of God, in denouncing hypocrisy and unrighteousness. There generally comes a time in the lives of all such men when something of the kind becomes inevitable. "*Liberavi animam meam*," and he is ready to depart.

Naturally he turned from the classes that rejected him to the little band of friends who trusted and loved him still. It is recorded that many of his most impressive discourses were uttered in the few hours that remained. It is not improbable, though we cannot be in possession of his actual words. The last days of a good man are very precious, and his last speeches are the most treasured. When a man anticipates a speedy death, while still in the full possession of physical and intellectual strength, it is only natural that the brevity of the hours should excite the intellect to unwonted activity. The treasures of his mind, won by years of meditation and deep experience, are poured forth without stint to loving and willing listeners.

Disciples press their questions, and would have nothing left unsolved.

The disciples at last realized the crisis. They had gathered together round the supper-table—had shared with the Master the meal which was the sign of the commencement of the feast they had come to celebrate. Then the Master told them how he had longed to meet them thus, how he had looked forward to that evening; it would be the last time he would be there. And so, said he, as the yearly feast comes round, as you meet at this memorial Supper, " Remember me!" How tender, how human, it is—this expression of the desire we all have to live for ever in the hearts that love us! Bidding them be comforted, in language which has since comforted millions, he prayed to Heaven for himself and them. The hour of death was nigh; and appealing from earth to heaven, he rose in thought high above the dishonour which the world was casting on him, to the glory God would give him.

But five short days ago, the sun had shone upon his entry into Jerusalem. The green boughs had hardly withered, the children's cries had scarcely died away, when he arose from the table and went out into to the night, to the anguish of Gethsemane, the mock judgment of the Roman governor, to Calvary and the Cross.

X.

THE END.

———•♦•———

WHY was he crucified? We cannot imagine in these days a man being publicly and ignominiously executed without some serious charge being satisfactorily proved against him. He must at least have been guilty of murder or high treason. We feel satisfied that Jesus was an innocent man, so we have to find out how some charge or charges, which must have been false, could have carried so much weight with the Roman governor as to have led him to assent to the crucifixion of Jesus.

We know Jesus only as a religious teacher, not only harmless, but one who was opposed to anything like sedition or violence. He was a simple missionary of spiritual religion, sympathizing with the religious cravings of the people about him, going about doing good, expounding the most fruitful principles of a pure morality, and speaking of the Heavenly Father in such words and tones as had never before been heard. Why, then, should such a man have met with a violent death? We have to recognize the fact that there were two parties to his execution—the leading men amongst the Jews, and the Roman Procurator, Pontius Pilate. The accusations that would have made the Jews condemn him, would not have had any weight with Pilate ; and the charges which would have led Pilate to sentence him, would not have mattered to the Jews. Let me make this clear. Pilate would not have cared if it had been proved that Jesus had violated the religious laws or customs of the Jews; it was no concern of his ; he had no respect for them, and he would have left the Jews to settle their quarrels amongst themselves. So the Jews accused Jesus to Pilate of sedition, of trying to stir up a rebellion against the Roman authorities, and make himself a king. Here Pilate had a right to interfere and judge. But after the examination of Jesus, he came to the conclusion that he was innocent ; he saw that he might be a religious fanatic, but he was not a rebel. But as the leading Jews, with whom Pilate wished to keep on friendly terms, persisted in their accusation, at last he took their word for the truth of the charge, especially as they threatened to accuse him to Cæsar, and gave Jesus up to be crucified.

But though this was the pretended offence of Jesus, it was not the real one. The Jews probably would not have been offended with the Galilean if he had

rebelled against the Romans; many of them had a
rebellious spirit; but it was the only accusation that
would justify an appeal to Pilate.

Amongst the Jews themselves, the charge was a
different one; they accused Jesus to the high-priest
of blasphemy and of trying to destroy the Law of
Moses. In a sense that charge was true, but in a
sense which only did honour to Jesus. We must
understand blasphemy merely as speaking against the
established religion and the practices of its professors.
A rigidly theocratic Church always regards this as
blasphemy. To speak against the Church or its priests
is the same to their ears as speaking against God.
Jesus had not spared the hypocritical Jews, and it was
this that enraged them against him. He exposed
their hypocrisy and cupidity, and they could not for-
give him. He had spoken against the Law of Moses,
because he had a higher law, the law of love and
mercy and inward purity, to preach. They saw that
his teaching was inconsistent with their system, and
that if all the people came to believe in him, the day
of the priests and scribes would soon be over. So they
determined by some means, no matter how unscrupu-
lous, to get rid of him; and the only way to do it was
to invent a charge of sedition and bring him before
Pilate.

Jesus understood their motives, fully appreciated
their malignity, saw they were determined to pursue

him to the death, and that no defence he could make
would save his life ; so he met their accusations with
indignant and contemptuous silence. When he was
brought before Pilate, the tradition preserved in the
fourth Gospel tells us that he broke this silence and
entered into conversation with the Roman governor.
Perhaps he felt that Pilate was not prejudiced like
the high-priest, and might understand his disinterested
motives ; though he did not much expect that Pilate
would acquit him, so he was not careful to explain
himself clearly. On the one hand were the princes of
Israel, as Josephus calls them ; on the other, was only
an obscure Galilean ; so he could easily realize what
the verdict would ultimately be.

Pilate began by trying to get Jesus to make an
admission which would justify him in condemning him ;
and repeating what had been said to him, he asked—
"Art thou the King of the Jews ?" Jesus said, " Sayest
thou this of thyself, or did another tell it thee ?" know-
ing very well that the Romans had not accused him.
Pilate evidently understood his meaning. " Am I a
Jew? Thine own nation and the chief-priests delivered
thee unto me. What hast thou done ?" Then Jesus
uttered his only defence. Playing upon the idea sug-
gested by the use of the word "king," he replied :
"*My* kingdom is not of this world. If my kingdom
were of this world, then would my servants fight, that
I should not be delivered to the Jews."

If he had been a rebel, if he had aspired to be king of the Jews, he would have raised an armed troop, and have defended himself against his opponents, and have fought for a throne. A rebel does not go about unarmed, followed by a few unarmed men and women and children. Those who set up for kings take a different course. It was as much as to say to Pilate : "Is not this sufficient evidence that I have not been guilty of sedition? What rebellion have I tried to provoke? My followers did not fight for me." Pilate would not or could not see his meaning, but seized upon what might verbally be construed into an admission, when Jesus said, "My kingdom is not of this world." "You are a king then?" Jesus answered, "You say I am a king ; but to this end have I been born, and to this end am I come into the world, that I should bear witness to the truth." Pilate was apparently convinced, but finally yielded and handed Jesus over to them to be crucified. And so ended that short and blameless career.

XI.

AFTERWARDS.

———·———

THE reader may say, "But that is not the end." To which I can only reply, That is the end so far as the life and teaching of Jesus of Nazareth is concerned. What followed is mainly a history of misconception, perversion and corruption. It is not the history of Jesus and his doctrines, but of the Church and its opinions. A strange, wild, incomprehensible story it is, too. It resolves itself into theology and history; but the theology cannot be disentangled from the history, the doctrines from the men who formulated them. It is the story of the conceptions and misconceptions, the agreements and rivalries, of nearly two thousand years. It is the record of saints and sinners, in which the saints are few and the sinners innumerable. It is the story of apostles and martyrs, of fathers and heretics, of hermits and monks, of crusaders and popes, of reformers and puritans. It is a record of lofty speculations and childish fables, of the tenderest humanity and the blackest and foulest passion. It is the story of the misdirected wanderings of a large part of the

human race for nineteen centuries; and the sequel is
the present almost mortal struggle of the most enlight-
ened inheritors of the Christian tradition to emancipate
themselves from the slavery of the past.

I have endeavoured to show, in the simplest and
briefest manner, that Jesus of Nazareth is entirely free
from any complicity in this melancholy aberration of
the human intellect. Its origins are to be sought, not
in Galilee, but in Egypt, Judæa, Persia, Greece and
Rome, and amongst the barbarians of the North and
West.

It appears to me that the religious teaching of Jesus
was as natural and unsophisticated as any that has
ever won the ear or touched the heart of mankind.
Faith in the beneficence of the unseen Power that
directs the course of human life and that supports and
fills the universe, and the obligation of gentleness and
mutual care and forgiveness among men, are scarcely
reducible to simpler terms; and these involve no doctrines and demand no ceremonies. That our conception of the world, guided by the light of science, is
vastly different from that of Jesus, does not affect the
principles of his religion. Love and trust have not
changed their nature, nor is their need less imperative,
nor the happiness they bring less certain now, than
they were in the days of Herod.

The gigantic institution called the Church, which
still rests as a crushing burden on the shoulders of

Christendom, is founded upon principles with which the Teacher had no concern, but which, on the contrary, he emphatically condemned ; and the hope of spiritual and intellectual freedom is bound up with its dissolution. The religion of the Galilean is concerned only with the experience and conduct, the hopes and fears, the spiritual and moral improvement, of the individual. The Church is a corporation, and is concerned with its interests as a corporation. The priests, the representatives of this corporation, are of necessity the enemies of freedom, progress and enlightenment— the conditions of that human advancement which in its natural course would lead to the abolition of ecclesiastical domination. This antagonism to sacerdotalism in its Jewish form was the natural consequence of the principles which Jesus grasped and preached, and his genuine followers must always find themselves in opposition to, and opposed by, the ecclesiastical organizations of their time.

It is in the hope of helping to break the yoke, so strangely composed of Jewish and other elements, which still oppresses Christianity, that I have written these pages. I have written also as an earnest lover of religion ; though not a religion of creeds, dogmas, sacraments and priests ; but a Natural Religion, such as Jesus found and proclaimed in the midst of the hills and fields and flowers of Galilee.